Under Orange Blossom

Poetry by Karishma Natu.
Illustrations by Ridi Hossain.

DEDICATED TO LITTLE KARISHMA.
you are a lighthouse of love.

segm

11

39

since i was a little girl
c a r a m e l
early   bird
1   .   5   %
s   t   e   p   s
on   the   table
only   if
31st   october

blossom begins

ripened

fallen from the tree

27

c a n d l e l i t
in   great   detail
flowers are for girls
eight in the evening
pit   stop
m   i   x   e   d
uncle's   place
the   22
papa,   my   eyes

home   or   away
all   that   for   a
underpaidleadingrol
on   delivered
dinner   date
roundabout   rive
s a t s u m a
simple yet profound

ents

romanticising
romance on a
rainy monday
covent garden stairs
if friendship
was a flower
pretty girl
s n a g
haven't planned
my outfit yet

peel and tear

49

59

stains

why do we put
b e n c h e s
beneath trees?
m o u n t
G O A T
promise, pyaar
amber at the lights
u n o - f u c k i n g -
switch, bitch
m o u t h w a s h
how to heal. asking for
more than a friend.

l e g a c y
curling goodbye
u n d e r
orange blossom
two ends meet
orange leaves
some day daughter
r o s e
sincerest apologies
share and tear

nectar

71

blossom begins

candlelit

chairs, chatter, *clinking glasses*

you stare at the candlelight flame like it's the most beautiful thing you've ever seen. notice if you care that it's temporary.

table for *two*

two plates either side

of kindle

s p i l l e d effervescent

laughter, **smiles** so big you couldn't fit them in your pocket.

if i could, i'd *cascade*

all over again like complementary wine. but you can't compromise with change.

by the end of dinner, talking fades to clashing of empty plates, cutlery crosses, chairs tucked. the candlelight sees it's way o u t .

you stare at the flickering embers. somehow it's still the most beautiful thing you've ever seen. notice how loving is culinary.

9

in great detail

my body is a still, silent statue.
an opera house inside.
home to the museum
of a plain old boy's bedroom,
beside other
shamefully hidden tour guides.
nobody pays to go in
and he's never there.
i keep myself entertained, i stare
at the trophies-
knowing that they, too,
made of shiny silver,
were made to be a reward
at the cost of their agony.

flowers are for girls

violets are her favourite.
they look pretty in her hair;
she looks pretty anywhere.

violets are her favourite.
they sit on the bedside table.
your eyes are now intertwined
but you don't know if you'd ever be able
to undress,
because you're thinking about the breasts
of a woman you've never met.

your lover turns toward the bedside table.
your head is tv static and hers
is drenched in dreams of maple.

violets are her favourite.
her father would get them for her every february.
if a man who i love did that, she thought,
then her days would rain with colourful confetti.

violets are her favourite.
but why pay attention when you can escape reality,
making love to a screen
as a sick substitute for intimacy?

violets are her favourite.
they look pretty in her hair,
she looks pretty anywhere.

eight in the evening

tomorrow, my movie muse drowns
beneath blue.
ocean waves curl like a set of jaws
         ready to indulge in one juicy bite,
               ripples for teeth,
                    and devour him for dinner.

         tomorrow, the sunset is celebrating
         the proposal of night and day.
         sky like lavender cake.
         an aisle of clouds meet marigold may.
         tangled in twigs, a fantasy
         glittering under a blossom tree.

today i am born again between page and pen;

where on earth will i be next week?

pit stop

daydream pitstop.
polluted in pink. too keen—
too ready for a twenty-something boy
face painted in masculinity,
with a god complex and an unscratchable itch
to feel seen.

what are you dying to tell me?
other than my "english is really good"
for someone born and raised in this country?
my urge to point every conversation towards philosophy
is my favourite thing to hate about me.
i can cook, i can dance, i can clean
(not for the archaic ideals within your family.)

lover girl. will spell your name in lockets.
build a landmark from the letters beside the sacre coeur.
make a living out of watching the world become a blur.

every box squashes me when i'm trying to fit in.

and i'm halfway to hierarchy
but i'll never have my mother's skin.
born to be a field of dalliance and daisies;
adorned as a crushed can thrown at the curb.

daydream pitstop.
polluted in pain. too keen.
i want to hide somewhere

somewhere i'll be seen.

mixed

horse walks into a bar.
bartender says,
       "why the long face?"

i go to christian school
at four years of age.
the kids say,
      "why the curly hair,
        the freckles,
          the black eyes, the black hair,
            the brown skin?"

i pray where i'm supposed to,
and people say,
      "why the curly hair,
        the freckles,
          the stained fingers
           on fair skin?"

i grew up in the countryside
at nature's request
believe me, if i could,
i would protest
to be made of one rather than two,

so i could be a top answer,
above a second-rate clue.

a horse walks onto an olympic marathon track
and the crowd roars,
        "wrong race,"

and i've lost count of how many times
someone has been inches away

               from saying that to my
face.

uncle's place

invited by lemon peel kitchen lights;
drawn in by semitones of spices.
it's cold but the rice and the music fills the room like
flame-kissed logs in the snow.
uncle hands me the kitkat he's been saving
and i savour it as if it were my last.

accompanied, marinated in companionship;
walls wallowing with poised plants,
blasting desi top forty,
feet shuffling upon kitchen tiles
better known as a dancefloor.

part of me ached for warmth,
even at a small age.
the living room sent me to sleep
in thick floral blankets
and incense that hugged my clothes
for longer than he was able to.

he walked in with tea
and a slice of the mint chocolate traybake he baked
but never tried for himself.
told me i took him to the cinema for the first time in years
to spill popcorn laughing at johnny english.
told me i should visit india, too.

as we sat watching sky movies with half full mugs,
i notice each ray of light in the room.
i notice the light that remained in his eyes.

noticed how i'd been colouring his days by number,
holding onto every last bite of wisdom he had.

the 22

tapping their watches as if time could drive in reverse,
as if i hadn't already been late,
as if i hadn't already made everything worse,

as if i didn't break down tens of times on the way.
my fuck ups pull in every hour,
and if it were anybody else, they could simply stop taking it.

---

my fuck ups pull in every hour,
and my family stand on duty,
waiting like late passengers beside the stop.

papa, my eyes

felt right.
hypnotised.
my love, my love, your eyes.

crowds like rippled waves,
two months no contact, no replies.
i'm in the station i returned to
one too many times
to try and say goodbye.

open a private tab:

what does it mean when he always makes you cry? I

for an orchestra kept composing
melodies only attainable
in your eyes.

why am i surprised?

despite my efforts i
was a fake excuse for a first
compromise.
a gorgeous little lie
you prayed would stay
stuck in the back of your throat,
and a love you let remain
burning on the backlog of your hopes.

because i was a gentle tide.
because as long as i could just about
breathe,
everything was fine

in my eyes.
just short of too long to recognise.
i could no longer look at you
without my insides curdling.
you walking, me hurdling-
the perfect recipe for disguise
having

a place in your life
is all i could've asked for.
i begged but belonged
squatting on the sill,
expecting nothing more than less.
window-watching half-genuine smiles
of celebrities you bumped into
and fake friends who swam in your success.

they don't know i gifted the smile
a little girl had been waiting to give
to somebody her whole life.

my love, my love grew.
stretched the corners of my mouth wide
to make room for you.
now your name pulls heavy on each tooth
because in return all you could do
was tiptoe around the truth-
they don't know you,
your what-a-waste-of-my-time yawning.
your revolting fascination,
my pretty-petal-like falling.

they remain oblivious
to your way of adorning
the bare minimum.
making it look so delicious.
bathing in your fame thirsty
persona.
i regret not pulling the plug
when i saw a sea in your eyes

that day.

to my father; i apologise.
you did not raise me
with such low expectations.
with a world warmed in your palms
to give willingly,
you gave me a continent
and i am so sorry.

not quite sure why
i sank so quickly;
deeper than the good i knew.
somehow my respect got tangled
between red skies
and the phase of 'honeymoon.'

now i'm left
traumatised.
smeared kajal.
tsunami across my waterline.
papa, papa, my eyes.

guys on film

he rents me
like an overplayed DVD.
mate, *don't tell your mum*
your favourite film isn't PG.
watch me confetti
your wedding with all your
text message receipts.

maybe
i'm petrified
of actually being loved,
or giving true romance a try.
i am treated like a trial
or trailer,
only to end up calling them for advice.

my excuses are scratched.
if his parents have plans,
that's my cue to get attached.

he rents me;
sees the five stars i have to offer
align,
saves it for the big screen,
only to take me back to the library.

placing me on the shelf,
as if i can't choose anybody else-
someone who could love me
for free,
not to be confined to TV.

fallen from the tree

since i was a little girl

turned head at the other half of me.
i'd like to give my sincerest apology
for being anything a person could dream.

i embody a tug of war
that is pulled   from two split
ends.
maybe at most i am deserving of
friends.

through the eyes of tradition,
i am nothing
but flu-ridden phlegm.

~~i am sorry.~~
that no matter how much
my middle overflows with creativity
and care,
no matter my grades,

what still matters is my shade.
what still matters is my cry into life.
i will never be good enough
                              to one day be a wife.

caramel

co-exist. the sun settles down.
co-exist. light happens before then.
summer's charm is around the bend.
free as kites fly. burned sugar on the stovetop.
blamed for mess-making. famous for it.
can a close eye create the most delectable caramel?

emulsify the right way. the sun must come up.
emulsify the right way. darkness must die before then.
day is just as night,
keep a careful watch on sugar and water.
keep tradition from searing, drizzle your sons,
slather your daughters.
caution creates the perfect caramel.

early bird

birds keep truth in their mouths
and freedom under their wings.
sorry for being too loud when i sing.

that house, the one in diu
my grandfather was raised in;
a village born beside sea
eventually wrung out with war,
painfully swollen with colonisation.

that house is a pitiful mystery to me
but if i had to imagine what it would be,
it would have pretty pillars
decorated in difference
spaced out to replicate the distance
between parted parent and child.
each pillar like the skin of an orange
in the spotlight of a sunrise,
carved out by the prices
my grandfather would have to pay
whether he prayed /
either way.

casted with the iron of disdain.
mouths are moving
uttering something about the
folded foundations and wilted walls
and the haunting conflict that remains.
raised a religion we must repent
with the back of our hands,
buried beneath our own shovelled sand.

a surname is a surname,
not just a birth certificate, but a brand.
they left me in total darkness
thinking i would never understand.

in the midst of red-handed honestly
hiding behind wings, i know
feathers fall only to repeat history.
i watched what was dangling from every bird's beak.
what would it have costed to show me?

1.5%

tucked up with a flag of white and green
i'm asking you to tell me how to feel seen
a farmer's pride, his puffed out shoulders
mother says i'll understand when i'm older

raised in a tearoom, cheddar and chutney
raised to believe i belong to one country
folks favour the luscious colours that spring has to birth
folks faint at the palette of faces god put on this earth

my father filled my lungs with his silent smoke
put a lighter in my pocket, sat back and watched me
learn to cope
as i walked in a village made of gasoline
so i could build a fire from the devonian dream

steps

my father's shoes
work harder than the rest.
soles tattered and torn.
still worn.

my father's shoes
sit exhausted by the door,
secrets stuffed into them like socks.

my father's shoes
have outlived pain
one too many times.

they have outrun war and
been broken in by poverty
all to make pathways for
places to call home.

they have walked tightropes
between devon countryside
and albufeira beach.

they have danced
to every kind of instrument
and stood in
every space of his silence.

they have walked me back from school
all the way to university dorms.

my father's shoes
sit exhausted by the door
and i ask
what i would have to do
to fill them.

on the table

strawberry fields
like hedgerow movie reels.
time makes a living out of your kind.
get all the good out of me, toss the rind.

proud mother and a praying son.
pressed father and a juice carton for a gun.
conditioned, concentrated, condensed.
scared to look at girls in the present tense.

straw chewer. suppressed milk teeth.
A-grade liar. high on dangerous dreams.
addicted to taking tears neat.

strawberry fields.
caught candid, read you real.
time to time to peace of mind.
squeeze out the good memories, toss the rind.

only if

across train tracks

across phone line, an easy act?
imagine decorating a home together,
two pairs of hands cutting the council tax.
across the bar of staying 'friends',
having no plans harvests hidden gems.
across sold out concert hall
across religious barriers, cultural walls
across sprinting mind marathon laps
flirting with the minded gap.
across distance staring me in the face
across;

yet always interlaced.

31st october.

my moles are pinpoints
mapping out the places my parents,
and their parents, and so on, were before.
my bronze skin a medal of survival victories.
my flesh rots like family hidden histories.

a child of the colonised.
a child of a coloniser.
a child of the sea.
a child of the free.
their mistakes etched onto me.
bus shelter. ugly graffiti.

you look at me like you could take me apart.
like i am a globe of puzzle pieces.
i look to you like it's a walk down the street.
you talk to me like i'm a monster.
i talk to you to feel half complete.

ripened

home or away?

do you want to love someone with a suitcase for a soul
or someone with a home for a heart?
do you want to love the source of inspiration
or the work of art?

one will pack up every moment spent with you and fly away.
one won't remember what it's like to leave you
because when you're apart they will find little ways to stay.

at some point you have to realise one of them was just a holiday.
while the other struggles to say goodbye even after a hundred different
delays.

all that for an underpaid leading role

my audition was a disaster.
i spilled everything all over the floor.
not just the flour but the four letter word,
left lingering like a neighbour's cat by the door.

my audition was a disaster.
picture a dancing damsel in cool girl trends,
summer kissed fresh fruit sliced too thin
and a top trump game of pretend.

papa said don't take risks.
don't burn alive just for people to see you exist.

my audition was a disaster.
i forgot how to perform;
half-remembered the rules of the game.
a mixed-race, pity-the-pretty-face shame.
spent the other half trying to conform.

my audition was rehearsed
for all of five minutes
staring at my reflection.
because where else should a diluted woman
seek a genuine connection?

commitment to a callback. a lifetime
of unwanted fame.
disaster after disaster.
a little girl's dream of dying
to end the life of her own name.

on delivered

i will keep your silences as folded invitations.

and in ten years, maybe more, i will open them, and only think
of anniversaries and occasions that could've
kissed the calendar if one of us had spoken.

dinner dates

dinner with my friends
spilling everything other than thai green,
glasses of tap water, or mugs of tea.
knowingly,
they say i "have a type."

a toothache; addicted to bad boys.
not really, just brown boys.
the type you think is your SRK,
until you realise he's playing you like the NBA.

the type where i dunk on 'em
with the biggest ego boost you've ever seen;
compliments and fucked-up-floral poetry
unread by a guy dressed for sports who
DING-DING-DING
wants to win but doesn't want me.

the type where they don't even shoot a shot,
because i'm wifey material but hmm; it seems like a lot.
so i'm at dinner with my friends
where i'm gushing once again.
dinner with my friends.
not dates with guys who are a five
scared to death when i put them at a ten.

roundabout river

we ebb and flow
over rocks parting meadows.

we glisten in daylight's gentle dance.
two swans and their craning necks, irrefutable romance.

we fall like rain on river
giving one flower life after being another's killer.

satsuma

that's the problem.
it's more than enough.
so much he can't bare.
so much a laugh lingers.
so much it is bursting

at every repeatedly stitched seam.
so much it is flooding the crossroads
guiding me to where to head next in life.

my arms are two paddles and they exhaust themselves
against the current. the love i have for him
is the weekend bag that i carry even on my working days.

never do i forget it's there; how could i?
it is brighter than the satsuma sun.
perhaps i could peel it if it was ever in reach.
perhaps i could share it with him.

simple yet profound

show at the door / please / rock your stupid tattered too loose jeans / spicy aubergine / peanut noodles / i miss you / how the fuck do you season tofu / anger has kept me on my toes / beautifully blistered / bravely bruised / being mean was the easiest thing to do / show at the door / speak soon / i've been strung by forbidden boys i'm / all out of tune peel and tear

romanticising romance on a rainy monday

a change.
bit of a crush.
a beating heart.
imagine a cherry blossom tree.
giggling, blooming– beneath
melted icicle sky, buttercream clouds,
and pirouetting petals of sweetpeas.

if he tied a bow in my hair,
looped pretty pink silk ribbon,
fashioned it around my curls:
he'd do it so gently.
it would be strong enough to stay but
loose enough that it wouldn't tangle.
march is where we began, incidentally.

did spring arrive with him?
applause from a live studio audience
after a long season of boo after boo.
sunlight tucked into his pockets,
laughed as he pretended to read my palms.

a sunday;
for a few hours, he is a sunray

but he could never be the season itself.
because spring is somebody else.
then i cry myself to sleep at quarter past twelve.
a change.
bit of a crush.
a sorry heart.
this path- the one where blossom
leads the way-

who does it lead to?

covent garden stairs

four hours and forty seconds ago,
          for just eight minutes,
               i fell. i'm not quite sure you could say it was love,
                  but for those eight minutes i stumbled
                      down 193 stairs; descended
                         into his sun-dressed eyes.
                              four daydreams and forty
lifetimes ago

                                        for
just eight seconds
                         our glances met before
our voices would ever get a chance.

if friendship was a flower

i picked a flower from the wild. decorated in daylight. caught in untamed beauty.
i plucked it from innocent stem. i put it in water. i put it in the windowsill. of course, it wilted. before, it was a masterpiece.

before, we were a masterpiece. until your name became pressed petals upon my breath over brunch with the girls. until we painted something breathtaking. an adventure tale of two. until we paint in soft spoken silence.
until we become an excuse for art. i'm sorry i picked you from the wild.

pretty girl

pretty little so and so
slipping like sellotape on satin
all things beautiful are borrowed
love is the new latin

lucky little such and such
like stray paper falling for a fireplace
when you've already got enough
why untangle longevity for lace?

pretty little so and so
anyone would think you're free.
but freedom doesn't give itself to
just one body.

snag

our souls catch like bangles on kurta.
our energies mingle, staying afloat like lotus
unbloomed, upon glimmers of gold in dusk-violet water.
sixty sand-grain seconds with you and not a single minute passes.
an entire day by your side and not an hour spent.

our gazes catch like candle wick catches a flame.
you look at me and your life falls like a theatre curtain.
as if you were free, and strong enough to love me
in some other lifetime,
just not this one.

i try to look at you without drowning.
i am no longer searching for God.
i am searching for a lifeguard.

haven't planned my outfit yet

date.
overnight pimple outbreak.
shrinking my personality
to squeeze into lack of originality.
so i become the size of a hair pin.

tucked under bass notes and ego strings
as rigid as a violin.
play a song now. play it badly.
fall for me stupid, jokingly, madly.

i am tired with being unattainable.
i am a lifetime of celebratory flowers and handwritten letters-
i am not occasional.

date.
close to calling it off
on the quest for fate.
close to being the girl
no longer defined by heartbreak.
a girl who looks the other way
a girl raised to wait

53

sta

ns

why do we put benches beneath trees?

trees will blossom, whether you want a ceremony of spring or the confetti of something you'd rather not celebrate or the heartbreak of it shrivelling and dying before you at the curb. blossom will fall. whether you like it or not.

tell me the gods didn't intent this to be so.

tell me they fought for millions of paths and i happened to keep crossing the one you say i " s h o u l d n ' t . "

blossom will keep falling on this path. not by choice, but by something no book could explain.

mount

a film of blood forms around our hands;
carving a secret religion from the lines on our palms.
we climb to the summit, cause chaos to find peace,
then bide time wondering why.

we happen to one another like winter happens to december.
i hike your impossibly steep mind;
your fingers stroll down the small of my back
politely, as if the blood wouldn't stain my skin.
as if the narrative looks like the end
but breathes like it's about to begin.

frost bites our tongues and catches us in a storm.
an indescribable blizzard. 'friendly' flurry.
we plummet down to cinnamon dusted dunes.
a film of blood coats our hands.
leave me down in the desert, finger paint on broken glass.
bury me beneath gentle sand.

GOAT

so– you're saying
after all the girls lined up
like sheep dotted on foothills,

mother's son, high in all his glory,
turns around
to see me,
goofy as a frost-furred goat
challenging gravity,
right behind him.

she told him stories,
dating back centuries

look at it!
no don't *actually* look at it!

those are **DANGEROUS**.
high on liberation- fun 'til you're dead.

what gets me is that instead
my father warned me about
about **limitations** loosening my head.

so–who's to blame?
the wind's soft echo up here,
or destiny's planned pivot of the foot?

all the girls
line up like sheep dotted on foothills
and you think by risking *my* life to
love him
i could've got him killed.

promise, pyaar

a year from now,
you are suited to someone
as blossom is falling from the trees.
a year of agnosingly
searching for pieces of you in other people
who never quite met my needs.
a year:
dancing with you in the park,
slow dancing with you in my dreams.
and the award goes to how easily you can act
like we were never meant to be.

belief is a hurricane but prayer makes it look like a breeze.
we are tripping on the wires of out-of-bounds memories.

a year from now, your bride will bring tears of joy
to the eyes i've seen through less than i'd have liked.
i take a back seat beside a fountain of french marigolds,
hung higher than my smiley disguise.
this time, our eyes won't meet.
though i presume they'd still battle busy crowds.
both of us are pathetic at being platonically tied,
and i am burning alive as you read your vows.

we became a tangle of unspoken what-if's and see-you-soon's.
maybe in one year, maybe in less, you will live with her,
and i will live with the fact that the best version of me
only exists when we are laughing
in the same garden or the same room.

provide her food and flavours i found,
memorise her go-to chocolate bar.
think of the snacks we shared,
pick her up in your family hatchback car,
promise me you'll wave her off
as if credits are about to roll,
whether she is steps away or somewhere far;

promise me, pyaar.
forget the numbness of being scared.
promise me, pyaar.
feel every pin, every needle. be good. be prepared.

i'll still know you like a tea towel knows a glass.
time will form puddles, time will pass.

a year from now, your wife will know you on the outskirts
with no sight of an end,
i'll no longer be a placemat for a proper plate.
but i'll still be your favourite friend.

perhaps life's greatest challenge is to wake up and pretend.

we cannot say goodbye. we are an impossible chance.
you are marrying someone.
i am still falling like a tree blossom's first dance.
a year from now,
the orange lodged in my throat bursts into flames
the universe explodes into stars
and i realise i was only ever simply a glance.

amber at the lights

you'll miss out on it.

moving far away
from everything your parents made.
your first pair of salt and pepper shakers.
how nimble, how unimportant.
yet how they season to taste.

staying awake to make sure she gets home alright.
turquoise lakes ticked by sunlight,
warm enough to dive into together.
echos of laughter living a hundred lives
recorded in ripples.

the bouquets
you might surprise her with once a week.
the things you could've said.
the crosses on the calendar
keeping a tally of all the days you could've met.

the way you looked at her as if
spelling your heart out, eye contact
overflowing with unconditional care.
the way you looked at her
in the same way the waves keep on rolling,
without blinking for air.

you'll miss out on it.
these things will pass you by.
she will search in all the wrong places,
only to settle for someone
who waits to watch her cry.

sometimes, you have to throw, even if you miss.
swim endlessly through crowds of faces
to see the smile you regularly reminisce.
because with her, you don't just stand there.
with her, you exist.
wouldn't it be a shame to miss out on it?

uno-fucking-switch, bitch

undefined goddess.
take out my hair pins;
puncture your heart.
take off the white jasmine
that dances around my bun;
adorn your neck.

unapologetic woman.
tear off this fabric;
tear your audacity to shreds.
my skin, glossed in gold,
is bulletproof.

your seeming sugary skin will scream,
limbs sent into spirals.
a sweetie to dispose of upon my tongue,
a little precious piping hot jalebi.

you've been praying for forgiveness.
i've been praying for a summer of solace.

mouthwash

stained your sharpened teeth
with syrup of seduction.
swam leisurely, polluted your arteries.
spiked your blood sugars,
revelled in destruction.

draped in daisy chains.
lips rich on honey butter,
skin drunk on vanilla cream,
stretch marks and growing pains,
roots drenched in jojoba and argan,
conversations killed by cookie cutters.

rinse, repeat. rinse, repeat.
say "AH" after savouring the sweet.
stained your sharpened teeth
with syrup of seduction.
a teaspoon or so for the time.
that's all you'll need.
that's all you'll ever search to find.

how to heal. asking for more than a friend.

southbank centre / lost key for the home we made / found a temporary renter / the way your grandmother softened paneer / tired toothbrushes / soft bristles / every i love you / sincere / yapped in confidence / ate in silence / muted the mundane / i rushed us violent / two sides to a coin / odd / 2 doesn't sit symmetrical on a page / with you / no costume / not with you / how to act on stage /

neo

tar

legacy

10:33.
square plates i wouldn't go for, personally
teeth marks in half eaten toast:
how could i love myself unconditionally
open your mouth, breathe for me

losing commas in conversation
they always try to see through
my stained glass eyes
trying to see inside
past the intricacies
and the powder pink blush pretty

"that girl is always doing something,"
says uncle shane.
truth be told i'd hate to watch my life
play out as anything close to tame.

10:33.
my name carries the legacy
of seeing love as success.
but how do you become successful
when the love you offer has no address?

curling goodbye

though we parted paths,
i will cling to the walls
of what we once had.

the thing that you now call "nothing."
is the thing that i visit daily like a patient.

a sorry hover in the hallway
of our almost accomplishments.

Under Orange Blossom.
Written by Karishma Natu

Silence seals them like two stems of a branch. The same unescapable smiles soften their lips. If the elephant is called in, it could cause an emotional avalanche. If not, it could put their friendship at risk of an eclipse.

HUGO (DAYDREAMING)

Imagine if we never had to leave…

JULIE

Imagine if this was all make-believe…

Hugo has to laugh. To him, the very idea that they exist at the same time is some kind of dream. Julie makes the time tick slow and Hugo's heart tick fast. Julie laughs like a summer scoop of ice cream.

A look of admiration pulls the two, yet something stays parting them.

HUGO (HESITANT)

Friends?

The elephant waits by the door. The could-be's try to go flat like loose-capped cola. The maybe's want more. Soon, the day is over.

JULIE (RAINED ON)

(pause) Friends.

FADE TO BLACK

two ends meet

don't come back now.
i have already had two years to i convince myself
that i am over you.
a downpour came in as if on queue
when i couldn't help but speak your name.
don't you dare laugh because you know

that we'll keep meeting under orange blossom.
and you hold a basket of small suns
that took all this time to grow
but we never have time to eat.
maybe we know they'll kill us,
we wouldn't be able to handle that kind of heat.

orange leaves

we are passing trains.
nothing more or less.
sparks ignite like fox tails
when we stop in our tracks.
our spirits wave through windows
but our bodies could never make the jump.

flowers clutter the station;
petals die like dust in my lungs.
it sounds so beautiful, but it hurts to breathe.
i'm embarrassed to build cities on paper,
i'm dreamt about for being so naive.
i've been stewing in spring for so long,
but i'd like to go home now.

i'd like to know what home means.

so when leaves
set themselves alight
at summer's last supper,
i will strike with the wind too
and burst
before your eyes.

when the funfair is shut down,
when we grow too old on the carousel of time-
i will stand right here in the middle of it all
and mouth goodbye.

orange leaves;
we stay where we are meant to be.

passing trains,
no more or less.

some day daughter

if i haven't learned to swim
on my own,
how could i save you?

if i can't harvest the life
i have tenderly grown,
how could i raise you?

i know i am capable of loving you,
but i cannot teach you anything
before making amends from my own four limbs;
arms like branches, so i can extend them
in need of your reach.

my best is not an achievement to obtain.
your best is a gift i'll never ask you to explain.

rose

a single pink rose.
following everywhere i go.
planted alone, picked specially
from a crowded meadow.

passed by on my walk around the neighbourhood.
spotted one in a park in paris,
breathtaking, and single it stood.
petals melting onto one another delicately
thriving dangerously, cascading irrevocably.

i almost felt sorry for them. i wished they could meet.
but roots are meant to home themselves
beneath soil, not to wander across cities and streets.

thought i'd seen this phenomenon before,
but these occasions felt real.
until after all, i stopped seeing the rose.
after all, perhaps it was just an ideal.

a single pink rose.
followed everywhere i would once go,
i'll never forget it,
not even in a meadow, or a million tomorrows.

sincerest apologies

silence / side salad / private emotional show / pity really / squashed scorpio / just messing / shamefully spicy / no dressing/ lovergirl vertigo / melt on the tongue / snow / wild western / young / divine feminine / unowned / being a woman is a lifelong olympic sport / going for gold / my straw short / her / pin-straight hair / truth over dare / forget me like a passing thought / love her like prayer/ papa how could he love me / i am freckled and half fair / armfuls of apology / not what you need / lack ingredients / to serve something pure / family to feed / tradition rocks the cradle / fuck me / can't say that / sorry /there's someone at the table/ who is able / let me be / delectable / let me / believe.

share and tear

open it.
orange peel mist.
split its cuticles, tear the fragile pith.

open it.
offer me a segment or three.
give me a hit of dopamine.
translate your love into vitamin c.

open it.
what we have cannot be reversed
it is final. it will colour our worlds.
then one day like the sun,
just upon the tip of the tongue,
it will

BURST

amb

82

rosia

lion's   den
l   e   g   s
c   r   o   c   h   e   t
traffic   lights
t   o   n   i   g   h   t
c   l   e   m   e   n   t   i   n   a
t   r   a   n   s   l   a   t   i   o   n   s
shy   with   you
m   a   j   o   r
d   i   l   a   r
if   the   miles   equalled   zero
universe   eyes

lion's den

bloodied dress / partner in love / lioness / mane untamed / to your dislike / to your distress

turned words to weapons / fought to be first / stronger than second / mouths to feed / bitches to beckon

legs

chairs were built to symbolise
power and prestige.
now they are made
so we can sit together.
so we can eat.

yet you choose defeat.
with hands like dog teeth
to a bone
i pick myself up
from scratch, from the floor alone.

chairs were built to belong at the table.
and though i sit on the floor,
i am not small.
why do you think the chair you sit so proudly on
was *made* to make ***you*** tall?

crochet

all the times i apologised for being myself
has left me an unwoven series of soft stitches.

i am trying to learn again; start from scratch
without tangling and tripping over loose ends.

it will be long- i think- threading loops,
undoing and redoing.

but i know that some day,
there will be a second pair of hands.
they will not hover at the ready
to pull everything apart.

a second pile of delicate squares.
a second stitch to inspire the third.

i know that some day,
just as i,
my crochet hook would've lived a life.

i know that some day,
even as we still learn how,
there will be a blanket.

traffic lights

my hair is laced in the scent of jasmine and a pretty bow.
sometimes life is a hat trick of green lights in a row.

i am beautiful by the coffee bar and i am brazen in the kitchen.
el takes the hot chocolate i made for her from my hand
before she asks what obscure combination of ingredients i'd like in my
sandwich, and after she stops to listen.

i'm talking and talking; bilingual in overthinking and under-acting.
i take a bite after she cuts my sandwich into two perfect triangles, and she
tells me to stop rushing.
the food is hot enough to scold me between two teeth.
"it's so GOOD," i say.
sometimes a minute can disguise itself as a day.

the sandwich el made took me an hour and ten trips to the kitchen to eat.
i caught a breath like a butterfly in a net for once.
i stopped in to see the view on a busy street.

my hair is laced in the scent of jasmine and a pretty bow.
sometimes life is a blessing in the form of a red light on a road.

tonight

tonight i decided that i deserve better
tonight
I
decided to grab the neck of my life's
outgrown t-shirt,
toss it and find something more fitting;
to notice myself and block boys allergic to
the concept of committing.

tonight I will take every pin they used to hurt
me to put my posture into place.
tonight I am spring in the soul and summer in the face.

yesterday I was just a dreamer;
tonight I am a believer
that I deserve better.
tonight,
the universe wrote me an apology letter.

clementina

a bakery's spinning smells
pirouette like ballerinas.
i am a galaxy of ingredients
and my recipe may always change.
it may always improve.

yesterday, i forgave the girl
who carried me here.
my love is a cathedral;
my light extends it's burned hands
and still emits from stained panes.

translations

no language exists
where i could possibly depict
the way i feel about you.
i'm listening to this lifetime
like my full-time job is to translate.

shy with you

timide? avec moi?
                                    oui
pour que?
                              je ne sais pas
tu n'as pas besoin d'etre
                          comment je peux etre sur
comment puis-je vous assurer
                          continue d'etre honnête
toujours
                          tres bien.

major

they said not to listen to your thoughts after midnight,   but your
name is a musical playing out in my ears.
like the sun showing its face after a long stretch of stars, your light became
the score to my life overnight.
there is nothing to be said about timing or tempo. notes always find
themselves on the scale,   never knowing when they'll find another in
harmony.

dildar

if the miles equalled zero

thumb wars / beauty mark tour / pass the salt / start a cult / pick our own pumpkins / find poetry in every puddle we jump in / alphabet soup / studs or hoops / belly laughs ricochet / spoon you like crème brulée / backpack / mundane / meld / butter flapjack / oil your hair / tuck in your chair / find flavour in ingredients we were blessed / no longer serve as special guest / break away from this test / alive in the autumn / without you now / my expectancy is shortened /

universe eyes

this orange

same magic made

you and i.

let's go halves on the universe.

let's settle like a linen sheet of stars.

call it ours.

good enough for two.

good enough for juice.

thought-full belly

misshaped; bruised.

muddied; imperfect.

made to desire fruits.

thank you to ridi for collaborating with me on this beautiful project. your love and support along the way has meant the world to me. i'm eternally grateful that i met you. never stop making art.

Karishma Natu is a twenty-two year old poet, born and raised in Devon, UK. During her time at Arts University Bournemouth, she hand-crafted two poetry chapbooks, which were shared with friends, family, and her community. Since graduating and getting her bachelor's degree in Creative Writing, she has created a growing space for her words on TikTok and released her first ever self-published poetry book in February, "Beneath the Blue."

Karishma wouldn't be herself without her headphones, latte art, and a hankering for french toast.

Karishma Natu © 2024

ISBN: 978-1-3999-9615-0

Socials:

Instagram– @karishmapoetry
TikTok– @karidaydreams